CYCLE A GOSPEL TEXTS

COWHERDING CHRISTIANS

SERMONS FOR
SUNDAYS AFTER
PENTECOST
(FIRST THIRD)

GARY
HOUSTON

C.S.S. Publishing Co., Inc.

Lima, Ohio

COWHERDING CHRISTIANS

Copyright © 1989 by
The C.S.S. Publishing Company, Inc.
Lima, Ohio

All rights reserved. No part of this publication may be reproduced, stored in a retrieval system, or transmitted in any form or by any means, electronic, mechanical, photocopying, recording, or otherwise, without the prior permission of the publisher. Inquiries should be addressed to: The C.S.S. Publishing Company, Inc., 628 South Main Street, Lima, Ohio 45804.

Library of Congress Cataloging-in-Publication Data

Houston, G. W. (Gary Wayne), 1943-
    Cowherding Christians / by Gary Houston.
      p.   cm.

    1. United Methodist Church (U.S.)—Sermons. 2. Methodist Church—Sermons. 3. Sermons, American.   I. Title.
BX8333.H63C69   1989   89-15748
252'.076—dc20   CIP

ISBN: 978-1-55673-128-0   PRINTED IN U.S.A.

Table of Contents

Preface			5
Lectionary Preaching After Pentecost			7
The Day of Pentecost	John 20:19-23	Where Are the Lilies Now?	9
The Holy Trinity	Matthew 28:16-20	The Doubting Sum	13
Proper 4 Pentecost 2 Ordinary Time 9	Matthew 7:21-29 Matthew 7:(15-20) 21-29 Matthew 21-27	A House for God	21
Corpus Christi	John 6:51-58	Misunderstanding Jesus	27
Proper 5 Pentecost 3 Ordinary Time 10	Matthew 9:9-13	Jesus' Hospital	33
Proper 6 Pentecost 4 Ordinary Time 11	Matthew 9:35—10:8 Matthew 9:35—10:8 Matthew 9:36—10:8	Cowherding Christians	39
Proper 7 Pentecost 4 Ordinary Time 12	Matthew 10:24-33 Matthew 10:24-33 Matthew 10:26-33	Studying under the Greatest Teacher	45
Proper 8 Pentecost 6 Ordinary Time 13	Matthew 10:34-42 Matthew 10:34-42 Matthew 10:37-42	Searching for Peace	51
Proper 9 Pentecost 7 Ordinary Time 14	Matthew 11:25-30	Come and Find Rest	59
Proper 10 Pentecost 8 Ordinary Time 15	Matthew 13:1-9, 19-23 Matthew 13:1-9 (18-23) Matthew 13:1-23	It Takes More than Sun to Grow	65
Proper 11 Pentecost 9 Ordinary Time 16	Matthew 13:24-30, 36-43 Matthew 13:24-30 (36-43) Matthew 13:24-43	Counterfeit Christians and the Rest of Us	71
About the Author			75

Author's Preface

It is a revealing thing to publish a book of sermons because it is a nakedness. None of us like to stand naked in front of others. Preachers are no different. Now my fellow and sister preachers can look at my sermons, criticize them, borrow from them, laugh with them. But maybe they will see one point that I try to make throughout many of these sermons: it is only by telling our own story that we have a sermon. As I share my story people can identify with my struggles and hopefully a few victories. Even though I shall never forget that one member of a congregation I served said that I talked about myself because I did not know "them." I do not think this is true, but anything can be narcissistic, sermons no less than anything else. I hope that some of these stories break down notions of "them" and "me." We are all on pilgrimages together if we are part of the Body of Christ. These sermons reflect then only one small part of that pilgrimage. I did not realize until I looked back on these sermons how much my Christian outlook has been shaped by childhood experiences of my father and in churches my father served. Most of these small country congregations are still going on — faithfully. Last Thanksgiving Day my father passed away and to his funeral came many people from congregations that he had served, many from decades back. The minister mentioned that "our works shall follow after us." They certainly do. We shall never know how much influence we have had on someone else. If we are fortunate all that influence will not be negative. My father has influenced my preaching and my life and so has the prayerful faithfulness of my mother, Margie Tharon Murphy Houston. That is part of my story, of who I am. Another influential person in my life has been my grandfather Pat Murphy who farmed those "southern Indiana hills." I can vividly picture my father standing in the pulpit as well as I can see my grandfather "down at the barn" or "out in the fields." Someone has said that a good writer writes about something that he or she has experienced. Another has said that good writing demonstrates universal feelings that all can identify with. I think that preaching is no different. Where mine falls down is not from lack of good examples from others. I have read and learned from the preaching of others. Sometimes I only learned what not to do. You might learn this from my sermons. But maybe, just maybe, you will find a good story or a new way of looking at a passage of scripture that you undoubtedly know as well as I. If this happens then this book will have been successful.

Lectionary Preaching After Pentecost

Virtually all pastors who make use of the sermons in this book will find their worship life and planning shaped by one of two lectionary series. Most mainline Protestant denominations, along with clergy of the Roman Catholic Church, have now approved — either for provisional or official use — the three-year Common (Consensus) Lectionary. This family of denominations include United Methodist, Presbyterian, United Church of Christ, and Disciples of Christ.

Lutherans and Roman Catholics, while testing the Common Lectionary on a limited basis at present, follow their own three-year cycle of texts. While there are divergences between the Common and Lutheran/Roman Catholic systems, the gospel texts show striking parallels, with few text selections evidencing significant differences. Virtually all the gospel texts included in this book will, therefore, be applicable to worship and preaching planning for clergy following either lectionary.

A significant divergence does occur, however, in the method by which specific gospel texts are assigned to specific calendar days. The Common and Roman Catholic lectionaries accomplish this by counting backwards from Christ the King (Last Sunday after Pentecost), discarding "extra" texts from the front of the list; Lutherans follow the opposite pattern, counting forward from The Holy Trinity, discarding "extra" texts at the end of the list.

The following index will aid the user of this book in matching the right text to the right Sunday during the "Pentecost Half" of the church year (days listed here include only those appropriate to this book's contents):

Fixed Date Lectionaries		**Lutheran Lectionary**
Common	*Roman Catholic*	
The Day of Pentecost	The Day of Pentecost	The Day of Pentecost
The Holy Trinity	The Holy Trinity	The Holy Trinity
Proper 4 *May 29 — June 4*	Ordinary Time 9	Pentecost 2
Proper 5 *June 5-11*	Ordinary Time 10	Pentecost 3

Fixed Date Lectionaries   **Lutheran Lectionary**

Common   *Roman Catholic*

Proper 6   Ordinary Time 11   Pentecost 4
    June 12-18

Proper 7   Ordinary Time 12   Pentecost 5
    June 19-25

Proper 8   Ordinary Time 13   Pentecost 6
    June 26 — July 2

Proper 9   Ordinary Time 14   Pentecost 7
    July 3-9

Proper 10   Ordinary Time 15   Pentecost 8
    July 10-16

Proper 11   Ordinary Time 16   Pentecost 9
    July 17-23

John 20:19-23 *The Day of Pentecost*

Where Are the Lilies Now?

Two years ago our family was on vacation. We drove up into the countryside near Bedford, Indiana to a small white church named the Mundel Christian Church. This is the place where I was baptized as a youth. At this pilgrimage spot of mine are fond memories of pitch-in dinners and all-day meetings as my father once held the pulpit there. But what remains with me more than anything is the fact that so many of my family members are buried there behind the church. The graveyard is big because the church has been there a long time. It stands silently reminding me that my grandfather, two of my uncles, my grandmother, a cousin, and my father are all buried close to one another.

As we visited that day we stood near the grave of my recently deceased grandmother. Then we walked over to the grave of one of my uncles. On his grave lay a single dead rose. This flower must have been placed there by one of the family after my grandmother's funeral. There was something sad, yet optimistic about that single, dead rose. From the seeds of dead roses grow rosebushes — with all their beauty. And our faith teaches me that none of my family really lives there in that graveyard.

Easter Sunday is always a time of great joy for the church. Preachers look out at swelled crowds. The pews are filled after the dreary winter, colored dresses and suits are everywhere. Children await the Easter egg hunt.

But, be that as it may — there is one thing we can almost always count on: there will be lilies in the church. Some may realize that the lily is a symbol of rebirth — of life winning out over death — of Christ winning out over death and Satan for us — of victory winning out over defeat.

We enter the Easter season after Palm Sunday and all the grandeur and majesty of Holy Week. Enthusiasm is running at a new high in the church — spring is here. The farmer is looking forward to preparing the fields for planting and is optimistic for a big crop. We start planning what to put in our gardens this year. Children are excited that school is nearly over. It is a time of new beginnings; a time of fresh possibilities. It is an exciting time! And do we ever feel good!

But then comes the Sunday after Easter and sometimes even the lilacs are gone. Do we still believe in the Resurrection after Easter Sunday? Attendance drops again in many churches and people begin planning their summer vacations. Our minds quickly turn from God to our own concerns. There is always the danger that we will put God in a chest until next year when we will get him out along with our new Easter bonnets and ties.

Now after Easter Sunday is a time that calls for increased prayer and a time of rallying around the empty cross and tomb. But instead we so often get on with other things. Do we still have the Easter excitement? Are we still excited about the Resurrection? In short, where do we go from here?

We are reminded of that first Easter in the church. The disciples were meeting together in secret for they were afraid of the Jews. Every knock on the door, every noise on the step, struck terror in their hearts. They feared that maybe they would be the next to die on the cross. You see, there was the strong possibility that they really would die. They were, after all, followers of the one known as the King of the Jews. They could be arrested and executed for treason against Rome. We are told that the doors were locked. We can almost see these disciples sitting there quietly, in prayer, fear, and sadness. They realized, all too well, that the one they had loved had been crucified. It looked like things were over. The adventure had ended. They had had such great hope. Then it happened! Jesus had been snatched from them and nailed to that cross. They were sad. Their hearts were broken. Their hope was gone.

Thomas was so depressed that he was off alone with his grief. Thomas had been off alone like a wounded dog licking a hurt leg. He had seen the lilies — at least for a few days. Thomas recalled the glorious entry into Jerusalem. He had heard the hosannas! The excitement had been intense — and then it happened! Jesus had died. Thomas had never understood this ending to the story. Imagine, for a moment, how Thomas must have felt. He had walked beside Jesus. He had sat near him. He had loved him and been loved by him. And now it was over. The bubble was smashed. The curtain had fallen. The only thing left was pain and an empty feeling inside. Thomas was not with the other disciples that first night when Jesus had come into the room and said to them: "Peace be with you." Thomas doubted their story about the Resurrection. He thought they were mad or making things up.

Thomas was not a bad person. He was like many of us — afraid to believe. Without doubt he had been disappointed many times in his life. What if this appearance of Jesus was a case of deception or mistaken identity? He could not risk being hurt once more. After being told that Jesus was alive, he said: "Unless I see in his hands the print of the nails, and place my finger in the mark of the nails, and place my hand in his side, I will not believe." I can identify with Thomas. Maybe some of you can as well.

We want to see God face to face and then believe! Our faith, at times, seems so fragile. I remember as a small boy telling my parents that it would have been easy to accept Jesus if you had seen him in person. Now I know that even that would have been hard. But imagine being with Jesus in a room and talking face to face with him. It is difficult to accept what we can not see. It is easier to believe when the lilies are here. It is easier to believe when the pews are filled. And it is easier to believe when everything is going well in our lives even if we do tend to forget God in those times.

Thomas was privileged to see Jesus in person after the Resurrection. Jesus said to him: "Put your finger here, and see my hands; and put out your hand and place it in my side; do not be faithless, but believing." Without needing to touch him, Thomas replied in some of the most powerful words of the Bible: "My Lord and my God." In my opinion Thomas had made the mistake that many of us make. He had stayed away from other followers when he needed them most — in his grief. If he had not been so wrapped up in his own sadness, he could have had his faith lifted by the community. The community could have supported and loved him. This is one reason to attend church. We share a common faith, not an individual faith alone.

From what looked like a shattered future a new vision arose among the disciples. Jesus breathed on them and said: "Receive the Holy Spirit." From that moment on they were not on their own. They were, and we are, sustained by this same Spirit to preach, heal and feed the hungry. We are to preach repentance for sins — the Kingdom is at hand. Now is the time to be excited and together! Jesus has called us blessed when he said to Thomas: "Have you believed because you have seen me? Blessed are those who have not seen and yet believed." You and I have not seen Jesus Christ with our physical eyes, but his presence is ever near us. And we can see his wounds everywhere we look in the world.

One learns to see better in time. If you are having trouble seeing with your spiritual eyes today — then I challenge you to spend some time with the other disciples. Do not stay away. We are called to love one another. And as we love one another we will uplift each other's faith in God. We will encounter Jesus Christ in one another. Let us remember that the lilies are here with us still. And remember, as the Body of Christ, we are his very hands and feet in this community and the world. Wherever we walk or whomever we touch proves once more the love of God and gives proof of the Resurrection of Jesus Christ.

Matthew 28:16-20 (L, C) **The Holy Trinity**

The Doubting Sum

When the eleven disciples, minus Judas, came to the mountain previously chosen by Jesus to meet him, some doubted. We would like to speak concerning the sum of doubt. Doubt adds up to zero. It is not a negative number; it is nothing! When we think of the word doubt we associate words like: indecision, uncertainty, hopelessness and powerlessness. People with convictions act. The opposite of doubt is faith and only faith has power.

Imagine the eleven, with the doubters included, hearing Jesus say: "All authority in heaven and earth has been given to me. Go therefore and make disciples of all nations, baptizing them in the name of the Father and of the Son and the Holy Spirit, teaching them to observe all that I have commanded you; and lo, I am with you always, to the close of the age." Do you see the irony? Doubting, weak people like you and me were given the Great Commission to make disciples of all nations. Talk about optimism!

Do you see how funny that is? Here are eleven people — some of whom doubted Jesus — and they were going to make disciples of all nations. That's ridiculous — yet they did it! It's almost as silly as a young lad imagining he can defeat a fully armed and armoured giant with a slingshot.

The only possible explanation is that the doubting sum was offset by the faithful sum. The faithful sum was a positive number. This is not too hard to understand since Jesus gives us the power to change from doubt to faith. He gives his followers the possibility to change into someone better. He gives us an open tomorrow.

It is estimated that the average American eats their own weight in sugar each year. The average is 150 pounds. This comes out to more than a teaspoon every hour, day and night.

Dr. Rudolph Ballentine in his book *Diet and Nutrition: A Holistic Approach* says:

> *When sugar is taken into the body, one's need for carbohydrate is satisfied. At the same time his hunger is eliminated. The very real need for other nutrients, however, goes unmet as sugar provides no protein, no vitamins, no minerals and no fat or fiber. It is a stripped carbohydrate and consists essentially of 'empty' calories. We might say that, nutritionally speaking, when one eats sugar he has incurred a 'debt'. . . Under a mountain of fat, many obese people are starving to death because they're not getting what they need.*

In other words people need substance — a solid food — and some settle for sugar which is only a quick fix. It is like that with real faith. It takes time, patience, and hard work to develop real faith. It does not come as a quick fix, or mushy feeling. Jesus wants to give us a total overhaul, not a patch-up job. He wants to eliminate the problem and open us the grace of possibilities.

Too many Americans either have two or three eggs, fried in butter, with sugary jelly on their toast, along with four or five cups of coffee — or else they have two or three doughnuts with this coffee. Then they feel guilty and have a chef's salad (ham and all) for lunch, and pizza for supper. These people wonder why they are overweight and plain don't feel good with anxiety and daily headaches. It is similar with all physical addictions.

We use too much salt, too much caffeine, too much sugar, and too much of several other things in our lives. If we want to change we must have the power to do so. Positive thinking is not enough. Bio-feedback is not enough. TA is not enough. We need simple faith working in our lives. We need action, not theory. We have to take the sum of doubt and add to that faith in a real, live, powerful Jesus who has said: "Go make disciples and teach them all I have taught you." It takes more than will power to change!

Maybe our church teaching has gotten out of whack. Years ago I was teaching in a university and I was approached several times by students who were seeking spiritual peace. I remember one young man, especially, whose name was Jerry. Jerry wanted to be baptized. He was worried about his eternal salvation, but he also wanted a new beginning. This new beginning, this fresh start, was symbolized for him in baptism.

All the young people had one thing in common. They had not had a positive experience in the religion of their mothers and fathers. These young people had gone to church, sung hymns, prayed, gone to Sunday School, and yet, they still felt powerless to cope with life. They were locked into old ruts and they wanted new spiritual perspectives that their local churches had not given them. They wanted to experience the spiritual adventure, not be taught religious dogma. They wanted more practice instead of more ideas.

Now don't take me wrong. I am not saying that all local congregations are bad. But I am saying that many seem not to know about the divine power that Jesus Christ has and how he wants to give us this power to live exciting, optimistic, open to change, faith-filled lives. Too many times we speak faith and practice doubt and criticism, whether of others or ourselves.

You see we must be open to change or else we have the narrowness of idolotry and not the adventure of faith. Christians can expect God to do the unexpected in lives. God will surprise us with hidden talents we never knew we had, new friends, new careers, new loves. Jesus Christ wants us to have power to abolish the sum of doubt. And we can!

How many of you see your life backwards? By this I mean you keep walking along the faithful path (slowly perhaps like a donkey), but all the time you have a crick in your neck from looking back at where you have been. Then you keep stumbling. Well, the answer is obvious my friend! Look where you're going not where you've been! Look ahead, not back. Everyone's made mistakes, so what?

We are certainly creatures of habit aren't we? We are addicted to things, feelings and ideas. One of the writers in the *Philoklia,* that classic of Orthodox Christianity, said somewhere that our own ideas are like children. We have produced them. We love them. And we protect them when these ideas seem threatened. In other words if we sense that someone does not agree with our ideas, we take this as a threat just as if someone had insulted or attacked one of our own children. So we are afraid of being wrong because we feel threatened in our very being.

I think we hang on to old, negative feelings because we are addicted to them. All addictions are not physical. We know these old faithless, negative ideas can't help us be any happier, but we are used to these ideas so we hang on to them. We would do almost anything to avoid the anxiety of change, even continue to be held by bad habits. We keep doing things that don't work because we don't know what else to do. We need new input.

I have a sign in my office which reads: "If you keep on doing what you've always been doing, you'll keep on getting what you've always gotten." Now that may not *sound* too startling, but think about it a moment. Let us apply it to an addiction, an old, worn out habit that no longer works, and see what it means.

I know a young man who has been "trying to quit smoking" cigarettes for years. He hates them. He knows they affect his wind and he wants to jog every day. And he simply hates to be addicted to anything. But he can't quit. Why? Because he's going about it the wrong way.

Each time he tries to quit he does it the same old way that he has already proven doesn't work! He tries to quit by sheer will power, which for him anyway, doesn't work. So after a few hours (or minutes) of "trying to quit smoking," he gets frustrated, or angry, or whatever so that he can have another cigarette. Then once again he has tried and failed and seems trapped in this negative habit. But this bad habit allows him to punish himself. Part of him wants to be punished and feel bad.

Now how does one quit smoking? You need to drink lots of water (to wash out the toxins), take vitamin C (to rebuild what the nicotine has removed), exercise (to lower the anxiety), eat properly, and have faith in both God and yourself. If you do this — you can quit. But you must practice, you must *act* as if you can quit. You can not look back constantly on how you have failed so many times in the past. If you do, you will be captured by doubt. Doubt looks back; faith looks forward. That's the real difference.

It is the same with diets. Diets do not work. You need to change the things you eat for the rest of your life, not just a few days. But you do this one day at a time. You give up ice cream and start to love apples. You cut back on pizza and substitute steamed vegtables. And you begin to see yourself as a loved person of God. Only if you love and acccpt yourself, just like you are, can you overcome an addiction, be it physical or mental. Addictions always have to do with low self esteem.

Our addictions, our fixes, are attempts to fill a void in our lives. This void of doubt and emptiness comes forth as a need for trust. If we are mistrustful of the world, if we are insecure, only a remaking will allow us to be full. We want love not criticism. We want action, not sermons. We want help. We feel empty and we want to be full so we try to stick some "thing" inside.

I have heard people who don't smoke say: Why don't you just quit? I have heard thin people say to heavy: Why don't you just diet? I have heard calm people say to the nervous: Why don't you just calm down? It is easy for us to tell others what to do, isn't it? But if you and I want to change we need help. This help comes not in a quick fix or a fad diet. It comes rather in a changed attitude. Change requires hard work and the ability to hang in there like the Christian in that old classic *The Pilgrim's Progress.* We have had enough of fads haven't we?

Somehow you and I want to change into faithful, dynamic, courageous Christians. How can we do this? Let me suggest a few aids:

1. Start looking forward, not backwards.
2. Concentrate on successes, even small ones.
3. See yourself as you would like to be. Believe Christ will help you become that way. Act as if you have already accomplished that change.
4. Try new methods to conquer old habits and addictions, not what has failed before. Do something different.
5. Set realistic, believable goals. But set thousands of them.
6. Get excited about change. See it as a real adventure of faith.
7. Read books by and about people who have accomplished what you wish to accomplish. Study what they do.
8. Pray about it. Ask the Lord for strength but believe he has already given it to you.
9. Look at what you are gaining, not at what you are giving up.

We must stop. Please remember that the sum of doubt is zero, or worse, a negative number! The sum of faith is living power in Jesus Christ. This power will give you and me the courage to change and free us from old ruts of negative thought and physical addictions. It will not be easy, but it is possible. It is this "possibility" that faith is all about. If you and I are going to teach all nations about Jesus Christ we are going to need power and energy. This power and energy is available if we but accept it. It is freely given. It can be freely accepted. Will you take it? There is a poem called "Stick With It" that says it well.

One step won't take you very far,
You've got to keep on walking.
One word won't tell folks who you are,
You've got to keep on talking.
One inch won't make you very tall,
You've got to keep on growing.
One deed won't do it all,
You've got to keep on going.

Matthew 7:21-29 (C)
Matthew 7:(15-20) 21-29 (L)
Matthew 7:21-27 (RC)

Proper 4
Pentecost 2
Ordinary Time 9

A House for God

I remember as a small boy sitting in a small country church with seats in auditorium style that you flipped up when you got out. Outside the window, where I sat, some wasps were buzzing around in the sunshine. From time to time one would fly in, then back out the window. People were fanning themselves with fans donated by a local funeral home; they had pictures of Jesus on them. My dad was preaching and he spoke of two houses, one built on sand and one built on rock. I could not understand why anyone, even a fool, would build his house on the sand. In Sunday school we sang a song that went: "The rains came down and the floods came up." I recall we moved our fingers like it was raining and the "house fell flat." Maybe you have heard the song.

Bedford, Indiana (my home town) is famous not for sand, but for rock. Bedford limestone is known all over the world. In the fields there are "outcroppings" of rock. I grew up knowing that rock would make a good house foundation; this rock had been good enough for the Empire State Building.

Have you ever thought about these two men in the story? One built his home upon "the rock," not "a rock." Not all rock is solid. The wise man knew this and built his own house — which was really his life — for God's glory upon good, solid rock. Rock just like I have seen so many times in Bedford.

When I think of sand I think of the many times I played in a sandbox as a child. I remember my cousin Janis had a neat sandbox. We would take our buckets, wet down the sand just enough to make it stick, and mold castles. It seems automatic to want to build sand castles, not houses. Castles are really grandiose houses, aren't they?

When I think of houses I remember our house being built out on Highway 58 near Bedford. Two carpenters worked for several weeks to build this house. It was built board by board upon a solid foundation with bedrock underneath it. The house still stands.

Across the street from where my father-in-law lives in Kokomo is another kind of house. This house, not having a solid foundation, is swaying. One of these days it will fall down. It is starting to look like dozens of old barns, garages, and sheds we have seen that are leaning, ready to collapse. They have foundations on sandy soil, not rock.

When I read that passage about the two men I recall the old hymn entitled "My Hope Is Built on Nothing Less." Here are the words of verses one and three that speak to illustrate Jesus' teaching:

My hope is built on nothing less
Than Jesus' blood and righteousness;
I dare not trust the sweetest frame,
But wholly lean on Jesus' name.

The chorus goes:

On Christ, the solid rock, I stand;
All other ground is sinking sand,
All other ground is sinking sand.

Here is verse three:

His oath, His covenant, His blood,
Support me in the whelming flood;
When all around my soul gives way,
He then is all my hope and stay.

Aren't those marvelous words? They're buried deep down inside me. I heard them so many times as a youth that I can never forget them. They are part of my very structure.

I remember when I was a guest preacher at a small country church in Miami County a few years back, I watched a man sing hymn after hymn without a book. He knew all the words. My foundation in Christ's church has been like that. How about yours?

I also remember night after night when my mother would read Bible stories to me. I'm sure the one about the two men who built houses must have been among the stories I heard. Still, though, I had the question: Why would anyone build their house upon sand? Are some people just stupid?

As I became older, and grew in my own Christian faith, I came to understand that the house on the sand was not necessarily built there from stupidity, but rather from carelessness. Some people don't pay any attention to the basic principles or the structure of their lives. They seem not to know that a solid foundation is necessary for a happy and fulfilled life.

There are many choices in life that face us. As we grow up we face various temptations: drugs, alcohol, smoking, gambling, stealing, dishonesty, sexual manipulation of others. There are many pitfalls facing the young person today. And these young ones very well might fall before one of these temptations for a time. However, if the foundation in Christ, the solid rock, is firm they will be okay. God will help them rebuild their lives to be stronger and better than they were in the first place.

How do you face the rains and floods of life? How do you get by when death strikes close, when jobs fail, when illness comes? Is Jesus Christ the foundation for all you do, say and believe? If not I bid you to get your house in order. Why not build a house for God? Your entire life can be like a glorious temple, not a sand castle, for God.

Charles Swindoll in his book *Living on the Ragged Edge* speaks of the unwise when he says:

> *Fools make all kinds of promises but they don't follow through. Through indolence the rafters sag, and through slackness the house leaks. Men prepare a meal for enjoyment, and wine makes life merry, and money is the answer to everything. Up above there are sagging rafters and a leaky roof. The house has been neglected because of procrastination. Even the courtroom of the king lacks fine appointments and disciplined servants because within the king's life there is an endless routine of nothing but food, amusement, plenty of booze, and stupid comments about money. In this case, the fools are saying to themselves, "Money is the answer to everything." That's a wasted time; there's a loss of priorities; there's a careless lifestyle; there's a lack of discipline toward unfinished tasks. Even though there are so many things to take care of, irresponsibility and verbosity abound.*[1]

The foolish person who builds a sand castle instead of a house for God upon the rock is not necessarily stupid. Rather he or she is careless. If you don't look after the foundation the entire structure will be shaky. It will sway under the influence of temptations' winds. Christians are challenged here by Jesus Christ to build lives upon him, not the sands of weal and woe. The circumstances of life change, but he is the same forever. He always loves us. Can you imagine that?

Now we have a small problem to discuss. Namely, we ask how do we get in touch with that rock? If our lives have been built on sand is it possible to start over and build a new house for God? I believe it is. I know it is. Sermons, instead of trying to make you feel guilty, should inspire you. The purpose of this sermon is to let you know that even if you have been foolish and have fallen from the flood — you still can start over. It's not too late to build a house for God with your life.

Did you know that God is good about that? The great preacher Harry Emerson Fosdick tells about his mental and emotional collapse in his book: *The Living of These Days* when he says:

> *For the first time in my life, I faced, at my wit's end, a situation too much for me to handle. I went down to the depths where self confidence becomes ludicrous. There the technique I had habitually relied upon — marshalling my wit and my volition and going strenuously after what I wanted — petered completely out. The harder I struggled, the worse I was. It was what I did the struggling with that was sick. I, who had thought myself strong, found myself beaten, unable to cope not only with outward circumstances but even with myself.*[2]

The house, we should say the sand castle, built by Dr. Fosdick collapsed. God tore it down with a flood. But you see there was a reason. God wanted a house built for him. Our God is a jealous God. He didn't want Fosdick's problems to be solved by intelligence alone. He wanted them to be solved by active faith in God.

Someone has wisely said that faith is not believing that God *can,* but that God *will.* Now hear these words again from his autobiography when Fosdick learned to turn his life completly over to God.

> *I learned to pray, not because I had adequately argued out prayer's rationality, but because I desperately needed help from a Power greater than my own. I learned that God, much more than a theological proposition, is an immediately available Resource; that just as around our bodies is a physical universe from which we draw all our physical energy, so around our spirits is a spiritual Presence in living communion with whom we can find sustaining strength.*[3]

The wise man has the rock to build on. The church we are told by Christ is built upon rock — the rock of faith. Our lives need also to be established securely or they will fall apart. Is your "life-house" leaning today? Do you feel like things are caving in on you?

If so why not consider a Christian remodeling job? It may be necessary to go all the way back to the foundation and begin again. I bid you to get in touch with the rock.

I am not giving you a list of shoulds and oughts. I am offering you instead a life with Christ with "can bes" and "possibilities" that only comes with faith and experience. The first step is to pray deep down inside yourself and find Christ there. He is the rock upon which you can build a house for God. How exciting that can be!

---

[1] Charles Swindoll, *Living on the Ragged Edge,* (New York: Guideposts, 1985), p. 307.

[2] Harry Emerson Fosdick, *The Meaning of Prayer,* (New York: Association Press, 1940), pp. 81-82, quoted in Wayne E. Oates, *Life's Detours,* (Nashville: The Upper Room, 1974), pp. 24, 25.

[3] *Ibid* p. 26.

John 6:51-58 (RC) *Corpus Christi*

Misunderstanding Jesus

Once a minister was speaking of the difference between fact and fantasy. "That you are sitting here before me in this church is fact! That I am standing here in this pulpit speaking is fact!" Then he paused, and continued, "However to believe that anyone is really listening to me may be fantasy." You know, sometimes it is fun to be a preacher.

After his return from church one Sunday a small boy said, "You know what, Mommie? I'm going to be a preacher when I grow up." "That's fine," said his mother, "but what made you decide to be a preacher?" "Well," said the boy thoughtfully. "Since I have to go to church every Sunday anyway, I think it would be more fun to stand up and yell than to sit still and listen."

Jesus was a preacher. And it is my contention that he was generally misunderstood by those listening to him. The people did not misunderstand because they were mean — they simply could not understand that God was doing something new through this strange Messiah. Let us back up to verse 41 right before today's lesson. This verse says: "I am the bread which came down from heaven." What did those listening to him say? They said: "Is not this Jesus, the son of Joseph, whose father and mother we know? How does he now say, 'I have come down from heaven'? " Jesus was speaking a deeper spiritual truth than those listening could comprehend. Jesus, the preacher, or anyone, can be misunderstood. Friends and family also often misunderstand one another. Those Jews listening to Jesus looked only upon the external. They asked how can he be the Son of God when we saw him grow up in Nazereth. "Even the gods," said the poet Schiller, "fight in vain against stupidity."

The Jews listening to Jesus could not see beyond the ordinary everyday. To put it simply they misunderstood Jesus because they had no poetic vision. They saw only a carpenter's son before them. They had no spiritual vision. Do you and I have spiritual vision, or do we also misunderstand Jesus?

T. E. Lawrence, a great scholar, was a close personal friend of Thomas Hardy, the well-known British poet. In the days when Lawrence was serving as an airman in the Royal Air Force he sometimes used to visit Hardy and his wife in his service uniform.

On one occasion his visit coincided with a visit of the Mayoress of Dorchester. She was bitterly affronted that she had to submit to meeting a common airman, for she had no idea who he was. In French she said to Mrs. Hardy that never in all her born days had she had to sit down to tea with a private soldier. No one said anything for a moment; then Lawrence replied in fluent French: "I beg your pardon, Madame, but can I be of any use as an interpreter? Mrs. Hardy knows no French."

A snobbish and discourteous woman had made a shattering mistake because she judged by externals.

There is a story about a rather arrogant young ruffian who frequented a cértain bar. One night a black man stopped in to use the telephone. The young man noticing him began to flip off smart comments at the black man. The comments got sharper and sharper. Since the black man paid no mind, the young man then began to get physically abusive. The black man simply smiled and walked out. As the young man walked back to the bar in a very cocky fashion the bartender asked him if he had recognized the black man. The young man said: "No! Why?" "Well I just thought you might have. That's Joe Lewis, the World Heavyweight Champion!"

I don't know whether the young man fainted or not. But don't we judge too much by externals, like those Jews listening to Jesus did?

The Jews listening to Jesus also were arguing among themselves. Jesus said to them: "Do not murmur among yourselves. No one can come to me unless the Father who sent me draws him; and I will raise him up on the last day." The Jews were so taken up with their private arguments that it never struck them to refer their decision to God. They were exceedingly eager to let everyone know what they thought about the matter; but not in the least anxious to know what God thought. But you and I should not be so quick to blame New Testament Jews for what we often do as well.

It might well be that sometimes in our committees when a man or woman is dominating and trying to push their opinion down other's throats that it would be better for us all to stop, be quiet, and ask God what he thinks and wants us to do. We need to discern the will of God in our lives. We misunderstand Jesus because we push for our own ways too often. The first step in understanding Jesus is to listen to him. The Jews listened to Jesus, but they did not learn.

There are different kinds of listening. There is the listening of criticism; there is the listening of resentment; there is the listening of superiority; there is the listening of indifference; there is the listening of the person who only listens because at that moment he or she doesn't have the chance to speak.

We will always misunderstand Jesus if we don't learn to listen. And we do *learn* to listen. Listening is an art that takes practice and experience to be good at.

If we read along in our gospel text for today we find that after this Jesus puts forth another hard saying. Let me quote it: "This is the bread which comes down from heaven, that a man may eat of it and not die. I am the living bread which came down from heaven; if anyone eats of this bread, he will live forever; and the bread which I shall give for the life of the world is my flesh."

The Jews misunderstood Jesus and asked each other; "How can this man give us his flesh to eat?" Jesus as the bread of heaven is both metaphor and fact. It is a fact that when we partake of Holy Communion we do somehow feed upon the body and blood of Jesus Christ. But it is mystery. When Jesus says: "I am the door," I do not see him as a physical door, but as the entrance into new life with God.

Jesus is the bread of heaven because he feeds us with his grace. His blood becomes our very pulse of life. When you and I gather to share in Holy Communion we are strengthened in body and spirit.

Truly we are *fed* by the body of Jesus Christ. And we realize that as we break bread, the body of Jesus was broken for each one of us sinners upon the cross of Calvary. But this scripture passage is not only about Holy Communion. It is about faithfulness to Jesus Christ as our Lord and Savior. Jesus is speaking here about "abiding" in him. By taking in his flesh we accept on faith who he is. And we abide, or remain faithful to who he is by keeping his commandments as 1 John 2:24 tells us when it says: "All who keep His commandments remain in Him, and He in them." So Jesus is speaking here of not only what he will do for the believer, but how in faithfulness the hearer demonstrates obedience.

This is important. It is not enough to get without giving. It is not enough to worship on Sunday and not through the week. We can rise every morning and renew ourselves to his service. This is what is meant here when our text says we feed on him and then he remains in us. And if we are to really receive from Christ what he has to give, if we are to have the experience of "saving power," then we need to feed on him. This means we completely absorb his teachings and his example. It means we appropriate his virtue until his mind becomes our mind and his ways our ways. It means that we stop and consider our actions and ask: "What would Jesus have us do here and now?"

When we are fed by Christ his power becomes our power until finally we can say like Paul: "I can do all things through Christ who strengthens me." Jesus has told us: "he who eats my flesh and drinks my blood abides in me, and I in him." This is clear.

Those listening to Jesus that day realized that a decision was called for. He pulled no punches and our text tells us that: "From that time many of His disciples went back, and walked no more with Him." People did not like nor really understand what they heard. The glib assertion thrown about that if only ministers would preach the "real Gospel" the pews would be crowded must be weighed against the history of Christ's preaching. Many of his followers left him because he preached a "hard sermon." Let us not give him less than all and misunderstand Jesus!

Some of those following Jesus had been drawn by the hope of having their material needs supplied. Others had been drawn to him in the hope that he would fulfill their national expectations. Few came because they felt the need of higher life and were convinced that Jesus could bring them that life. Only those drawn to Jesus by the Father, who truly understands, will stand when the going gets rough.

Let us understand! To understand means literally to "stand under." Let us stand under Jesus. To know Jesus Christ means to serve him. You and I are called to service, not to privilege. In serving him we find ourselves. Let us not misunderstand Jesus . . .

There are then, to sum up, two basic steps required of us. We must first stop and listen to what the voice of God is really saying. We must not make it say what we want it to say. We must lay aside prejudices and preconceived notions of God's plan for our lives. We must live the adventure of faith into the unknown.

And, secondly, after we learn to understand Jesus we must be obedient. It is not enough to simply understand him. We must obey him or else we cannot call ourselves his followers.

A soldier doesn't only wear a uniform and march in parades. There comes the day he must fight.

You and I are called to be soldiers of Christ's holy cross. What a marvelous, awesome privilege we have. May we be worthy of the task Jesus Christ has set before us.

Matthew 9:9-13   **Proper 5**
Pentecost 3
Ordinary Time 10

Jesus' Hospital

Our Holy Gospel for today says that "as Jesus passed on from there, He saw a man named Matthew sitting at the tax office. And He said to him, 'Follow Me.' And he arose and followed Him." Now that's what we call a response to a call don't we? Jesus said: "Follow Me." Matthew got up and followed him. The problem with many of us is that we haven't even gotten up yet, much less are we following Jesus.

Jesus Christ empowers us to come follow him, but we have to get up and start moving as Matthew did so many years ago. Matthew, by the way, means "Gift of God" in Hebrew. Strange when you think of it, that one with such a name would be a tax collector.

Tax collectors were hated by the Jews because these toll masters were seen as turncoats, mercenaries, if you will, who worked for Rome against their own people. In Tibet, when the communist Chinese forces took over in 1959, many Tibetans collaborated with the enemy. They were hated. We all know what the name Benedict Arnold evokes in us.

William Barclay says in his commentary on Matthew that "no man ever had such faith in the possibilities of human nature as Jesus had." He saw something in the face of this one called "God's Gift" that the others could not see. Jesus saw one who would get up and follow him.

> *Nelson's Illustrated Bible Dictionary* makes a good point when it states:
>
> *By His attitude toward the tax collectors, Jesus showed that God's covenant of grace extends to all people — not simply the righteous who observed the law of the Old Testament. In fact, His message was that God would welcome the repentant and humble tax collector, while He would spurn the arrogant Pharisee . . . His mission was to bring sinners — people like the tax collectors of His day — into God's presence.*[1]

Now what did Matthew do after this call? He was so happy he threw a party! He invited all his tax collector friends and all the sinners to come to meet Jesus. Matthew wanted to bring other people into Christ's presence as soon as possible. Notice that he did not try to convert others by bright logic or clever words. No! He brought them to meet Jesus personally.

This is what many of us need today. We need a deeper, personal relationship with Jesus Christ. We don't need gushy devotional talks. We need soul searching prayer where we come into Jesus' Hospital for healing like Matthew did. Now Matthew did something that many of us haven't done. He brought all his friends into the presence of Jesus, which we can call Jesus' Hospital.

The other day I had to go see my doctor. I was having blinding headaches every day which I assumed, and he confirmed, were sinus headaches caused by the recent heat and high humidity. I was sitting in self pity when I heard someone struggling with the door to come into the waiting room. I heard something clank and in came a woman dragging an oxygen tank behind her on a little cart. She gasped deeply, with a rattle, for several minutes because fighting the door had worn her out.

I went in to see the doctor, got some prescriptions, and when I was walking out I saw another older woman sitting there with her head down in her hands in complete dejection. She looked very depressed and I do not doubt felt much worse than I did. Another lesson about my self pity struck home.

When the Pharisees questioned that Jesus ate with tax collectors and sinners, what did Jesus respond? He said: "Those who are well have no need of a physician, but those who are sick." The he added: "But go and learn what this means: 'I desire mercy and not sacrifice.' For I did not come to call the righteous, but sinners, to repentance."

We do not know too much about the medicines used in Jesus' time period. We have all heard of the balm of Gilead, which some say was an aromatic substance taken from an evergreen tree. (A guess, by the way!) And we know that wine mixed with myrrh was used to relieve pain by dulling the senses. This mixture was offered to Jesus upon the cross. But apart from this we know very little about early Hebrew medical practices.

However, we do know about that Great Physician named Dr. Jesus who healed at that time and still heals today. Sometimes he heals the soul and not the body. Sometimes he heals both. And Jesus is the only doctor I have heard of who bleeds himself instead of his patient. We are healed by his wounds and his blood.

Have you ever heard of the ichenumon? This is a small weasel-like animal that can overcome and destroy a venomous snake of over a yard long. It is said that this animal will only attack a snake when it is near a certain plant whose leaves contain an antidote for snake bite. When bitten, the little creature immediately retreats to the life-saving plant and nibbles its leaves. It is then restored and ready to renew the attack. Each time it is bitten, it goes to the plant and then returns to fight the enemy.

Perhaps one of the reasons some are not healed is that they have gone too far away from Jesus, the Tree of Life everlasting. We need to eat his body and drink his blood and become restored. This takes a response to his call: we have to get up and follow him. We have to go where he lives and leave behind all those tables of things that keep us bound. Matthew left his tax table and went to eat at the Lord's table. Should we not do the same? I think yes!

Thomas Watson once made some observations about Jesus, the healing Physician, and said that Jesus came to heal us not because we desired him, but because we needed him. Watson also said that many are not healed because they do not know they are sick. This is similar to those with psychological problems in that they rarely admit to a problem.

The Pharisees did not know they were sick in their self righteousness. There are many who come to church and when they hear the word sinner immediately think of a neighbor, or perhaps the preacher — but never themselves. Matthew knew he was sick. He knew he was incapable of self-healing. He had made money, but that left him still sick. So he put his confidence in Dr. Jesus.

Today you and I are invited to Jesus' Hospital for a thorough soul check up. We need a treadmill test to see if our hearts still have any love left in them. We need to plug our emotions into a tester and see whether they go out to others or get blocked up with a tourniquet of self concern.

There was a story published in the *Gospel Herald* that said:

> *Dr. Howard A. Kelly was a renowned physician and surgeon, and also a devout* practicing *Christian. During the summer holidays when in medical school Dr. Kelly sold books to help with expenses. Becoming thirsty, he stopped one day at a farmhouse for a glass of water. A girl came to the door. When he asked for a glass of water, she sweetly said: "I will give you a glass of milk if you wish!" He drank the cool, refreshing milk heartily.*
>
> *The years passed, Dr. Kelly graduated from medical school, and became the chief surgeon in the John Hopkins Hospital. A patient, one day, was admitted to the great hospital. She was from the rural area and was seriously ill. She was given special care, being placed in a private room with a*

private nurse. The skilled chief surgeon spared no effort to make the patient well. After undergoing surgery, she convalesced rapidly.

One day, she was told by the head nurse, "Tomorrow you will go home!" Though her joy was great, it was somewhat lessened by the thought of the large bill she must owe the hospital and surgeon.

She asked for it. The nurse said, "I will bring it to you!" She brought the itemized bill. With a heavy heart, the patient began to read the different items from the top downward. She sighed. But as her eyes lowered, she saw the following notation at the bottom of the large bill: "Paid in full with one glass of milk!" It was signed: "Howard A. Kelly, M.D."

That is like it is with Jesus. He has healed those who have responded to his call. And he will heal those who will yet respond to that call. And the best of all is that Dr. Jesus, the head physician in Jesus' Hospital, has paid all the bill for healing himself even though the price was very high. Our healing has been paid for with draughts of his blood. Alleluia, he died to heal you and me.

If you don't know about Jesus' Hospital, why don't you come inside and check it out? Let Jesus examine your soul and heal all the hurts and worries that you have.

---

[1]*Nelson's Illustrated Bible Dictionary*, ed. Herbert Lockyer, Sr., (Nashville: Thomas Nelson Publishers, 1986), p. 1033.

Matthew 9:35—10:8 (C, L)
Matthew 9:36—10:8 (RC)

Proper 6
Pentecost 4
Ordinary Time 11

Cowherding Christians

I don't know about you, but I have difficulty identifying with the image of Jesus as the Great Shepherd. This is not said to be negative. I simply have no experience with sheep. I was around cows for a couple of years though. Therefore, today I would like to talk to you about "Cowherding Christians."

My grandad was a farmer and for many years he had milk cows. I can close my eyes and almost see him today heading out across the field in his old Chevy truck, rounding up the cows. True, he didn't dress much like a cowboy, but he brought home the cows nevertheless. Some of the cows would stray and he would have to go "round them up." Most of the cows, however, simply walked on toward the barn when it came near milking time. They did what they were used to doing and since seven days a week they were milked twice a day they got used to the routine.

Going back even a few more years, I can remember two dogs my grandad had at different stages of his life. The first dog had been named "Butch." The second was called "Ring." Both dogs could round up the cows. Butch was the best though. Butch was so good that he even knew which cows had gone dry and which ones still gave milk.

My grandad would send Butch out and say "Go get'em!" Smart dog, huh? If I tried that with our Pomeranian I don't think much would happen, except that Sugar Baby would go hide under the bed and growl at me. You see, she is my wife's dog and not suited for cowherding.

Maybe, therefore, it would be better for me if Jesus had said: "Go to the straying cows and bring them to the barn. Go get'em!"

Now you might be thinking that this imagery is strange. But in some ways humans are much like cows. Some just wander around looking for greener grass. Or they follow the same old trails they've always taken.

We are one big mass of humanity now. Our moods and interests are very much influenced by television and advertising. Few of us often think orginal thoughts or do daring things. It's easier for us just to ramble on, never quite reaching the barn. What we need today are more cowherders, of good quality of course.

Have you ever been to New York City or Los Angeles or Chicago? Besides all the cars, what you notice are the thousands and thousands of people all frantically trying to get somewhere other than where they are.

Toki Miyashina wrote a modern version of Psalm 23 that is appropriate. It changes the image of the Lord as Shepherd into the Lord as Pacesetter.

It goes like this:

The Lord is my pace-setter, I shall not rush:
He makes me stop and rest for quiet intervals,
He provides me with images of stillness,
which restores my serenity.
He leads me in the way of efficiency,
through calmness of mind;
and His guidance is peace.
Even though I have a great many things to accomplish each day
I will not fret, for His presence is here.
His timelessness, His all-importance will keep me in balance.

*He prepares refreshment and renewal
in the midst of activity,
by anointing my mind with oils of tranquility;
my cup of joyous energy overflows.
Surely harmony and effectiveness shall be
fruits of my hours
and I shall walk in the pace of my Lord,
and dwell in His house for ever.*[1]

Jesus told his disciples: "The harvest truly is plentiful, but the laborers are few. Therefore pray the Lord of the harvest to send out laborers into His harvest."

The first lesson taught by this Scripture is that all good works should begin with prayer. Too often people pray as a last resort. "There is nothing left but to pray" — we sometimes hear said of the sick. Or we hear people say things like: "I've tried everything, guess it's time to pray."

Our Lord, on the other hand, instructed his disciples to begin their activity with prayer. "Pray the Lord for laborers," he said. Why go to prayer first? Because it reminds us, right up front, that the seed is the Lord's, the fields are the Lord's, and the harvest belongs to the Lord.

The Lord felt so strongly about prayer that he taught his disciples the famous prayer which Protestants call today "The Lord's Prayer" and the Catholics call "Our Father."

John Wesley felt strongly about prayer, as well. He once wrote a prayer that went like this:

Fix thou our steps, O Lord, that we stagger not at the uneven motions of the world, but steadily go on to our glorious home; neither censuring our journey by the weather we meet with, nor turning out of the way for anything that befalls us.

The winds are often rough, and our own weight presses us downwards. Reach forth, O Lord, thy hand, thy saving hand, and speedily deliver us.

> *Teach us, O Lord, to use this transitory life as pilgrims returning to their beloved home; that we may take what our journey requires, and not think of settling in a foreign country.*[2]

Friends, what most of us really want is to get safely home to the barn at evening feeding time. And our Lord has not only identified with us in his compassion, but he has sent ministers, teachers, evangelists, choir directors, Sunday school teachers, musicians, and many others to minister to us and to feed us along our journey. His love is so immense for us!

But who did the Lord chose as his very first disciples? Did he choose saints, unlike ordinary men? No! He choose people very much like you and me. They were laymen, unlearned, plain and yet believers with gifts he saw that he could use to further his kingdom. Notice, however, that he chose them. They were not simply volunteers. You see we all have different uses to our Lord. And Jesus knows best how to use each one of us.

There was a pastor named Alexander Maclaren who used to tell of a man who attended where he preached. This man was very intelligent and so Dr. Maclaren preached a whole series of sermons dealing with various intellectual difficulties concerning religion and life.

To the doctor's delight, the man came shortly afterward and said he had become a convinced Christian and he wanted to join the church.

Overjoyed Dr. Maclaren asked: "And which of my sermons was it that removed your doubts?" "Your sermons?" said the other man. "It wasn't any of your sermons. The thing that set me thinking was that a poor woman came out of the church and stumbled on the steps.

"When I put out my hand to help her, she smiled and said 'Thank you' and then added, 'Do you love Jesus Christ my blessed Saviour? He means everything to me.' I thought about what she said. I still have some intellectual difficulties, but now He means everything to me, too."

Jesus took rough, common, unlearned men with their stumbling faith. He took them with their brooding doubts and their grievious sins and made them his friends and co-workers.

Jesus even gave Judas every chance He could to enter the kingdom. He said things in Judas' presence like: "A man's life does not consist in the abundance of possessions." However, Judas chose thirty pieces of silver over eternal life with God. Tell me now, aren't some of us dumb as cows? I wonder this morning how many of us are ambling down old familiar lanes that lead everywhere except to the barn? Where has your life been leading thus far?

A Sunday school teacher was examining her pupils after a series of lessons on God's omnipotence. She asked: "Is there anything God can't do?"

There was silence. Finally, one lad held up his hand. The teacher, disappointed that the lesson's point had been missed, asked: "Well, just what is it that God can't do?" "Well," replied the boy: "He can't please everybody."

Jesus ministered to the masses. However, he never pandered to them. We can not water down our beliefs to be accepted by everyone. Nor do we help anyone when we try to please all. Jesus Christ died in order to set us free from the power that sin has held over us. You will not read in the Bible that he approved of sin. But we find over and over that although he does not approve of sin, he loves sinners. If you and I are to be counted among the harvest, we need to pray for others, have compassion for the lost, and zeal for the Lord's glory. Prayer reminds us what we are about. Compassion reminds us that others are like us. Zeal reminds us that Jesus Christ works miracles through small people.

I remember praying one special day in a church a few years ago when I did not feel my sermons were helping anyone. I looked up at a stained glass window to see a picture of Jesus there with a small lamb in his arm. And I heard clearly an inner voice saying: "Feed my sheep." Well, I guess that settles it! I would rather be a cowherder. But if Jesus wants me to be a shepherding preacher, a pastor of a small part of his flock — so be it. What does he want you to do? Why not pray and find out?

---

[1]Toki Miyashina, "Psalm 23 for Busy People," *Eerdman's Book of Famous Prayers,* compiled by Veronica Zundel, (Grand Rapids: William B. Eerdman's Publishing Company, 1983), pp. 114, 115.
[2]John Wesley, "This Transitory Life," *ibid,* p. 64.

Matthew 10:24-33 (C, L) *Proper 7*
Matthew 10:26-33 *Pentecost 4*
  Ordinary Time 12

Studying under the Greatest Teacher

Robert Frost's first assignment for a class of teachers was to read "The Celebrated Jumping Frog of Calaveras County." This was Mark Twain's famous story about a frog that lost a jumping contest because he had been pumped full of quail shot. When the class next assembled they were mystified because they did not understand what this story had to do with a course in education.

Frost patiently explained to them that this particular story was about teachers. He said that there were two kinds of teachers. There was the kind that filled you with so much quail shot that you could not move and the kind that gave you a little prod on the behind so that you could jump to the skies. I am very fortunate in that I had two such teachers who did not only fill me with buckshot.

I worked with a man named Dr. Helmut Hoffmann for nearly five years in graduate study at Indiana University. At that time I was involved in Comparative Religions and Tibetan Studies. It was my intention to become a great scholar like Dr. Hoffmann. He was quite well known for his academic prowess in Europe and the United States as well. He knew over twenty languages that I was aware he knew. He had studied English, German, French, Italian, Tibetan, Latin, Greek,

Hebrew, Sanskrit, Nepali, Mongol, and Manchu to name only a few. He believed that one could not become a serious scholar without a command of the proper research tools, and he had little good to say about superficial American education. So like him I embarked on the study of German, French, Russian, Tibetan, Mongolian, Sanskrit, and a few others. It took years and I am still studying. Some now call me a polyglot, or even worse. But you see I imitated my teacher. I wanted to be like my teacher. He was my model for living.

Since Dr. Hoffmann was a Buddhist I also learned how to meditate — just like him. I meditated upon the four elements: earth, water, air, and fire. I chanted mantras that I had learned in Sanskrit as I focused my eyes upon a candle and learned to control my breath for longer and longer periods. I remember like it was yesterday attending Tantric services that Dr. Hoffmann recited in Sanskrit. But I was not cut out to be a full fledged Buddhist, although I still value meditation. There came that time when God called me back to him through Jesus Christ and a call into the ministry.

After a long struggle of several years I reaffirmed my Christian faith and accepted that call. I will never forget how disappointed and stunned Dr. Hoffmann was when I told him that I was going to enter seminary that fall. He sank down into his chair, put his head between his hands, and said: "Then it has all been for nothing." I felt sorry for him. I knew his pride was hurt and he felt that I did not learn the important thing from him: to become a Buddhist. But I did learn many things from him. And I did accept his advice to finish my Ph.D. Even today when I do scholarly articles in that field I do things according to "Hoffmann's Method."

One autumn I entered The School of Theology, an Episcopal seminary in Sewanee, Tennessee. It was then that I met my second great teacher: Urban T. Holmes, III, who was Dean of that seminary. Terry, as he was affectionately called by those of us who grew to know and love him, was also a great scholar, teacher, and friend. He inspired me with dazzling theological discussions and with his high level theological books.

Although he has been dead now for several years I am still Terry's student as well as Dr. Hoffmann's. I still read their books over from time to time. And, as with Hoffmann, there was that time that I wanted to be just like Terry. I edited and published two serious books on interfaith dialogue, probably in imitation of Dean Holmes. I tried my hand at heavy theological writing and found I had little talent. But I learned something from both these great men — and that is to be myself and reach for the skies.

Now I am called a lay person's theologian and a preacher. That is fine. I do not want to write books that people cannot understand. Instead, I want to preach clear sermons that proclaim Jesus Christ as Lord and Teacher for all who choose to say yes to him.

What then did I learn from these two teachers? I learned that I could be more than I had thought I could be. And I learned that all great things take much work. And under their inspiration I accepted a renewed position under that greatest of all teachers Jesus Christ.

As Per-Olof Sjogren wrote in his little book *The Jesus Prayer:*

> *We live in a world where we can choose. I can believe in God even if no one else does. I can pray to Jesus at any time, wherever I am, and no one can prevent my doing so. This is my freedom of religion. Jesus is my master, not all the forces that assail me, trying to make me think as other people think, believe as other people believe, and do what other people do.*

Jesus has told us in Matthew's Gospel: "A disciple is not above his teacher, nor a servant above his master. It is enough for a disciple that he be like his teacher, and a servant like his master. If they have called the master of the house Beelzebub, how much more will they call those of his household." What does this mean? It means what thousands, perhaps millions of Christians know we are called not to privilege, but to service.

Every year when the North Indiana Conference of the United Methodist Church meets at Purdue I see twenty to thirty people receive their Elder's Orders. I look into the eyes and see youthful optimism in some, mid-life career changing in others and even angry, defiant glares in others. But I also see a saying yes to Jesus Christ as that ultimate teacher for them.

Don't we all say this first yes from our immaturity and also often from selfish motives? I know that I did. I wanted Jesus to help me to direct my life, to give me a central focus. Why then should not these getting ordained do the same?

I have now been in the ministry for eleven years. That is not a long time, but I have seen that most people come to church, at least in the beginning, to get something. People even express this when they say things like: "I didn't get anything out of that sermon." Most preachers hear something like this from time to time — some of us more than others. I believe that since I hear that so often Jesus must be trying to teach me humility. Just kidding! No, not about the humility!

So we turn to Christ for selfish reasons! We turn to him in our pain or loss, in our search for meaning, in our loneliness, but that is what God wants us to do. He wants us to come to him, sinners that we are. We do not have to do anything first to get ready to follow this teacher. We do not have to finish undergraduate studies first.

However, there comes the time, really many times, when we realize that to get to that crown we have to carry a cross first and die. We have to die in order to find eternal life. Strange, perhaps, but that is how God set it up.

And, what is more, we find out that we do not die just once. We die over and over again. Most of my own deaths have been painful ones. I died screaming. I still do. I say things to God like, "Why is this church so low in attendance?" He says "Wait!" I get discouraged and threaten that I will give up just any day now. He says "Wait!" Then he adds: "Gary, I still love you."

Have you ever had any feelings or fears like I have had? I have been discouraged, attacked, threatened, misunderstood, bored, elated and surprised on my spiritual journey and I keep on dying. Perfection certainly takes a long time doesn't it?

George Maloney has written:

If we wish to enter into an ever increasing awareness of loving union with the triune God, then we must expect a lifetime of dying to self-centeredness. We must surrender to God's complete control on all levels of human existence. This means that the love of God is discovered and experienced to the degree that we empty ourselves of all that may impede a total surrender in trusting love to God.

May I submit that the main obstacle to our spiritual growth is the fact that we identify with our egos instead of with God living in our hearts? Jesus has said: "Therefore whoever confesses Me before men, him will I also confess before My Father who is in heaven. But whoever denies Me before men, him will I also deny before My Father who is in heaven."

I know that I deny Christ in many ways. I deny him with empty words. I deny him with silence by not speaking up when I know that I should. I deny him with unfaithful actions.

One person has asked: "If you were arrested for being a Christian would there be enough evidence to convict you?" I ask myself that question. How would you answer that question?

In his mercy Christ allows our pride to be cut down, our egos shoved over, and our hearts to grow. And I thought that as I shared this intimacy with you that maybe you could see yourself in some of my own struggles and deaths. Perhaps, like me, you also are not perfect yet. Maybe you find yourself in pain or see some part of yourself being dismantled.

Perhaps you have been rejected by someone you have loved. Maybe you have had a recent significant loss in your life. Whatever may be going on, please know that Jesus was deserted by the very disciples he loved and taught. Jesus suffered temptations and overcame them. Jesus died like we will die. He understands you wherever you are and however you feel.

But we must see that being a follower of Christ is not an easy journey. He said that we must leave all to follow him. Maybe even your family is divided and your husband or wife is not a Christian. Jesus said that it would be so. You will be persecuted, rebuked, argued with, called names, and perhaps even killed for his name.

But Jesus has promised that all who confess him before others, will he confess before the Father. I believe this. Do you? Is so let us be faithful and imitate that "Greatest of All Teachers." Remember that they called Jesus names. In fact, they called him Beelzebub, the devil. Jesus knew though that these names could not change who he was and is — the Son of God and our Teacher.

Matthew 10:34-42 (C, L)
Matthew 10:37-42

Proper 8
Pentecost 6
Ordinary Time 13

Searching for Peace

The motto of the Apollo II flight was "We came in peace for all mankind." This phrase was upon the plaque deposited on the surface of the moon. The flight had landed on what is known as the "Sea of Tranquility." Armstrong and Aldrin found a tranquil and peaceful scene on the moon because there had never been any humans there prior to them. No one before them had had a chance to disturb the moon.

As I was preparing this message I asked my teenage daughter what the word "peace" meant to her. She replied directly and quickly: "No war!" This may not be a very positive definition, but when you stop and think about it war is easier for us to visualize and describe than peace. We have more experience with war, and it definitely makes a more exciting movie background for television shows than does peace.

Ministers Research Service has concluded that since 1919, the nations of Europe have signed more than two hundred treaties of peace. Each treaty, simply another scrap of paper, was broken more easily than consummated. From the years 1500 B.C. to A.D. 1860 more than eight-thousand treaties of peace, meant to remain in force forever, were concluded. The average time that they remained in effect was two years.

In his address to the United States Senate in 1919, President Woodrow Wilson said, "The League of Nations is the only hope of mankind." How futile and tragic such hope has proved to be! At this very moment the United States Navy is providing military escort to Kuwait oil tankers. It is a vain attempt to stabilize an area torn by war. And if you notice movies on Vietnam are becoming popular. Our world knows much about war and little about peace.

Every year at Christmas time we sing "Peace on earth, good will to men." Then by New Year's Day we realize that little has changed. Can there be no peace? Don't we call Jesus the Prince of Peace?

Look at your own life. Do you find peace there? Maybe you thought it would be more peaceful when school was out for you and you got a job. Perhaps you were waiting to retire or for the kids to grow up and move out. Maybe you are looking forward to, or recently have had, a vacation. Do you now have peace?

We are reminded of the people who take vacations to find peace, then drive hundreds of miles, spend thousands of dollars, and still have a miserable time. Or let us consider those who buy "hideaways" only to find that they now have to drive up to the lake each weekend if for no other reason than to cut the grass and check to see that no one has broken in. Is that peace?

And then there are some people, of course, who do obtain a level of peace in their lives only to find it boring; you see we do not like the same, old, peaceful thing day after day.

Let us ask ourselves some questions, if we are not depressed enough by now. Is peace really the aim of Christianity? Is it the main object of the Christian religion to give you and me an undisturbed and placid life? Is that actually our goal?

It is not an undisturbed life that we want. Rather we realize that to live means to endure and overcome, to aspire and to attain. We obtain satisfaction in life not from "doing nothing," but rather from accomplishing life goals and spiritual goals.

The person who settles back and thinks that his religion has ever done its work on him because he is at peace may not understand what life or religion is all about. This does not mean that there are not plateaus where the thrill of accomplishing something benefits our state of mind. But peace does not mean doing nothing, it means being content with what we do. In the middle of a storm the clouds can be pretty.

It is not the best thing for a person to receive his religion ready-made, to ask no questions, and to be free of wonder. This is not peace. This is laziness! Instead we are challenged over and over again to stretch and grow beyond our complacency into more and more of what God intends us to be. In a strange way peace is connected with growth. Peace is an attitude of openness and reaching out and forward.

In one sense Jesus brought no peace at all. He was a revolutionary. He rocked the social order of the day while he ate with sinners and outcasts. He had a concern for the poor that the religious establishment lacked. Those who thought they knew that religion was about rules and such did not enjoy Jesus telling them that the spiritual life is involved not with rules, but a general outlook on life, a certain attitude. Jesus did not do it right for them because he did not teach what they in their closed minds thought was religion. As a result of this there was certainly no outward peace in the land.

Jesus said that he came not to bring peace, but a sword. He came to divide families. He came to ask people to take up a cross and to follow him even to the death if necessary. Jesus came to employ a spiritual judo by allowing weakness to overcome strength.

Jesus also attacked traditional theology with its lists of what one should do or not do. It is most unfortunate that much of modern Christianity has fallen back into this aspect of dogma. Aldous Huxley says in his book *The Perennial Philosophy*:

> *It has been fancied that souls are saved if assent is given to what is locally regarded as the correct formula, lost if it is withheld . . . To suppose that people can be saved by studying and giving assent to formulae is like supposing that one can get to Timbuktu by poring over a map of Africa.*

Religion at the time of Jesus consisted in committing catechisms to memory and in proof texting from the *Torah*. Christ came with a different message of salvation by grace and freedom in him. He spoke with paradox and metaphor. No wonder there has been and still is little peace in the church. Unlike Jesus, we do not always foster independent thought, nor do we always set our priorities straight. As one man has said, if a "heretic" is what the dictionary tells us it is — a man who gives forth his own opinions when they are in conflict with the received opinions of his age — then there never was such a heretic as Jesus the Christ.

Jesus taught that one did not need to simply recite the books of Moses and the prophets. Rather people were expected to act "in the spirit" of love and to have faith like Abraham that could move mountains. Faith in Christ is not the same as faith in dogma. Jesus taught that he did not want faithful dogma, or correctness of view — whatever that is — but rather faithful people.

It is not too far from the mark to say that today some people want peace at any cost. We run from conflict. We want unanimous agreement in our committees even if it means letting an ego maniac run things. We seem, at times, to be more afraid of what people think than concerned with what God desires. Whatever happened to good, old-fashioned fear of God?

You and I do not need peace if it means complacency and stagnation. Rather let us have war! Let us have war against self-centeredness and the power of the ego! Let us have war against nice churches that fail to preach and practice the power of the liberating Gospel.

Let us have war against self-righteousness, that sin above all others that Jesus attacked. For it is our own self-righteousness that keeps us from hearing the Gospel of love for sinners. Let us open our churches to those of different attitudes and different ideas and learn from them instead of fearing them. The power of truth will prevail we need have no fear.

William Barclay in his commentary on Matthew relates a story about

> a lad in a country village who, after a great struggle reached the ministry. His helper in his days of study had been the village cobbler. The cobbler, like so many of his trade, was a man of wide reading and far thinking, and he had done much for the lad. In due time the lad was licensed to preach.
>
> And on that day the cobbler said to him, "It was always my desire to be a minister of the gospel, but the circumstances of my life made it impossible. But you are achieving what was closed to me. And I want you to promise me one thing — I want you to let me make and cobble your shoes — for nothing — and I want you to wear them in the pulpit when you preach, and then I'll feel you are preaching the gospel that I always wanted to preach standing in my shoes."

That is a marvelous story of self-giving. But we do not need to become sentimental. We need rather to rediscover the militant nature of the Body of Christ, not from a position of supposed moral superiority, but from a loving concern to spread the Good News. Too many of us have retired without ever having been on the front lines. Too many of us have never done very much at all and we are tired already.

But there is a peace that passes all understanding that comes even to the Christian warrior. This peace comes by allowing Christ to give us, in his love and grace, a still center in the middle of the world's strife. This peace is reinforced as we turn to pursuing a life of service to our King. We can be at peace with God even if the world turns into shambles.

There are basically two ways of living: for self or for God. The first one brings despair and emptiness. The second brings the peace that passes all understanding. These two views are contrasted so sharply in two particular poems that we will use them to close. The first poem is part I of "The Hollow Men" by T. S. Elliot (although you should know that later in life he reaffirmed his Christian faith) and the second is entitled "What I Live for" by George Linnaeus Banks. T. S. Elliot might have been the better poet, but we prefer the words of comfort found in the second poem. The poem by Elliot reads as follows:

We are the hollow men
We are the stuffed men
Leaning together
Headpiece filled with straw. Alas!
Our dried voices, when
We whisper together
Are quiet and meaningless
As wind in dry grass
Or rats' feet over broken glass
In our dry cellar

Shape without form, shade without colour,
Paralyzed force, gesture without motion;

Those who have crossed
With direct eyes, to death's other Kingdom
Remember us — if at all — not as lost
Violent souls, but only
As the hollow men
The stuffed men.

Now for the poem by Banks:

I live for those who love me,
  Whose hearts are kind and true;
For the Heaven that smiles above me,
  And awaits my spirit too;
For all human ties that bind me,
For the task by God assigned me,
For the bright hopes yet to find me,
  And the good that I can do.

I live to learn their story
    Who suffered for my sake;
To emulate their glory,
    And follow in their wake;
Bards, patriots, martyrs, sages,
The heroic of all age,
Whose deeds crowd History's pages,
    And Time's great volume make.

I live to hold communion
    With all that is divine,
To feel there is a union
    Twixt Nature's heart and mine;
To profit by affliction,
Reap truth from fields of fiction,
Grow wiser from conviction,
    And fulfil God's grand design.

I live to hail that season
    By gifted ones foretold,
When men shall love by reason,
    And not alone by gold;
When man to man united,
And every wrong thing righted,
The whole world shall be lighted
    As Eden was of old.

I live for those who love me,
    For those who know me true,
For the Heaven that smiles above me,
    And awaits my spirit too;
For the cause that lacks assistance,
For the wrong that needs resistance,
For the future in the distance,
    And the good that I can do.

Matthew 11:25-30 *Proper 9*
Pentecost 7
Ordinary Time 14

Come and Find Rest

Salvidor Dali, the famous artist, reported that when he needs a short nap, he puts a tin plate on the floor. Then he sits on a chair beside it and, holding a spoon over the plate, relaxes into a doze.

As he falls asleep, Dali relates, the spoon slips from his fingers, clatters onto the plate, and he snaps awake. Dali claims that he is completely refreshed by the sleep which occurs between the time the spoon leaves his hand and the time it hits the plate.

We really do need rest from time to time don't we? I remember that years ago, when I worked in a certain factory, we would get two breaks before lunch and two after. It seems like many breaks to some, but if you have a monotonous job, like I had, you need breaks. We also need breaks from our lives.

Jesus would withdraw from his teaching and healing every few days and would go off to be alone. He would spend entire nights in prayer, but I imagine that sometimes he simply rested. It could be that he stopped and enjoyed the beauty of the flowers or gazed off from a hill top into the valley below.

Resting does not come only from going to bed and sleeping. As Oswald Chambers writes in his spiritual classic *My Utmost for His Highest:*

> . . . *"And I will give you rest," i.e., I will stay with you. Not — I will put you to bed and hold your hand and sing*

> *you to sleep; but — I will get you out of bed, out of the languor and exhaustion, out of the state of being half dead while you are alive; I will imbue you with the spirit of life, and you will be stayed by the perfection of vital activity. We get pathetic and talk about "suffering the will of the Lord!" Where is the majestic vitality and might of the Son of God about that?*

The fact remains that many of us fail to obtain necessary rest from daily tasks. I believe that a major problem with both clergy and laity is burnout. For example, one person serves on committees for year after year then comes the time that he or she is completely exhausted and "retires" from all church work. Rest is needed.

I have seen several pastors suffer from burnout. It is such a common problem that there are now quite a few books on the topic. Burnout means loss of zeal for life. Burnout means nothing brings pleasure anymore. The only cure for burnout is rest, sometimes a change of scenery, or maybe a change of attitude. But burnout does not mean that one need remain inactive for the rest of one's life.

In the Kewanna, Indiana, weekly *Observer*, publisher Bill Lyon ran this notice on page one:

> THE OFFICE OF THE *OBSERVER* WILL BE CLOSED JUNE 1, 2, AND 3 DUE TO GOOD FISHING CONDITIONS. THE OFFICE DOOR WILL BE LEFT OPEN AND PAPER AND PENCIL WILL BE ON THE COUNTER FOR ACCOMMODATION OF PATRONS WHO WISH TO LEAVE NEWS ITEMS OR ADVERTISING.

This is a man who knows how to rest! But is this what Jesus really meant when he said: "Come to Me, all you who labor and are heavy laden, and I will give you rest?" No, Jesus was referring to his Jewish audience that was burdened with all the observances of Mosaic law. These people had regulations on their food, clothes, how they farmed, and so on. The taxes were overpowering. To these people Jesus said: "Come to me. Stop being burdened by law and accept your salvation by grace, the grace that I give you."

These words speak to us as well. They speak to us when we try to merit heaven by our good works. They remind us that we are saved by grace through faith. These words point us to Jesus, not to "works righteousness."

These words remind us that Jesus Christ died on the cross for the sins of all who will say yes to him as Lord of their lives. These words tell us that we can stop worrying about "doing it right" and can rely on his grace and love instead. We can rest in Christ's love.

Matthew 12, verses 29 and 30, speak to this: "Take My yoke upon you and learn from Me, for I am gentle and lowly in heart, and you will find rest for your souls. For My yoke is easy and My burden is light."

Jesus challenged his hearers to come and work with him, be yoked with him and then the labor would grow easier. A budding artist once painted a picture of the Last Supper. He took it to the famous writer Tolstoy for his opinion. Carefully and understandingly the Russian master of words studied the canvas. Then pointed to the central figure, he declared: "You do not love Him." "Why that is the Lord Jesus Christ," exclaimed the artist. "I know," insisted Tolstoy, "but you do not love him. If you loved him more you would paint him better."

We can learn to love him better, but we have to be truly yoked in service with him. Jesus used a beautiful symbol: a wooden yoke. Yokes were used in order for oxen to pull plows and wagons. These oxen were beasts of burden, of service to their lords. Everyone standing in the presence of Jesus that day would easily picture in their minds what a yoke looked like and how it was used.

The *Interpreter's Dictionary of the Bible* had this to teach about yokes. "The carpenter probably made both yokes and plows. Joseph and Jesus undoubtedly had experience in making yokes."

William Barclay makes the following statement in his commentary on Matthew:

> There is a legend that Jesus made the best ox-yokes in all Galilee, and that from all over the country men came to him to buy the best yokes that skill could make. In those days as now, shops had their signs above the door; and it has been suggested that the sign above the door of the carpenter's shop in Nazareth may well have been: "My yokes fit well." It may well be that Jesus is here using a picture from the carpenter's shop in Nazareth where he had worked throughout the silent years.

The brilliance of Jesus' preaching is evident here. He took a symbol, well known to his hearers, and gave it a new twist. He was saying — and is still saying to us today — subjugate yourself to Me. Put on My yoke; submit to My authority and find rest for your souls.

Jesus gave us the example of service when he submitted himself to the authority of his Father. He asks us to do the same. But, yet, he adds another dimension here. He wants us to take half of the yoke and put it on our shoulders while he takes the other half, the heavy half, and wears it himself. That gives me a marvelous feeling because I know that I do not have to face all the problems of life alone. Jesus is with me. And I know that he is with you as well. But you and I have to let him be with us. One man has written: "They spell 'relief' when they have a case of acid indigestion or heartburn and they spell out R-O-L-A-I-D-S . . . wouldn't it be nice if we could find relief from all the problems and anxieties of this life simply by swallowing a tablet?" He goes on to explain his own spelling for relief: J-E-S-U-S.

Let there be no mistake. Jesus has sympathy for your condition, and after all you have done or failed to do, he still says come to him. It is you he means. He knows about how you are. He knows the trials you have had. He knows your heartaches. He knows the personal losses you have experienced.

And he says come. He says come and lay all this slavery to the world and its burdens down at his feet. He challenges you, nay, he pleads with you, to come rest in him. We cannot doubt the sincerity of Jesus when he promised to give us rest. We only need believe in him and he will do what he has promised.

You and I can let go of our sins. We can even let go of our egos and die to ourselves in order to live in him. Jesus wants to help all of us. Sometimes it is only our pride and self-will that keeps him separated from us. He must have our cooperation, but you and I are learning about that, aren't we?

Matthew 13:1-9, 18-23 (C) *Proper 10*
Matthew 13:1-9 (18-23) (L) *Pentecost 8*
Matthew 13:1-23 (RC) *Ordinary Time 15*

It Takes More than Sun to Grow

A father and his son went for a ride on a trolleycar. The boy seemed to be completely absorbed in the passing sights of San Francisco. His father, feeling a bit mischievous, lifted the boy's cap from his head and pretended to throw it out the window. The boy began to cry, so his father whistled and placed the cap back on his son's head. He made believe that he was able to bring the cap back by a mere whistle. The lad's tears disappeared and he laughed. "That's fun," he said, "let's do it again" — and he grabbed his cap and threw it out the window.

That my friends is like a parable. It cannot really be explained — or the joke loses its point. You either get it or you don't. You can not explain a joke. The same goes for a parable. That being said, let us now explain a parable.

A parable has, first of all, several layers of meaning, but it strikes each given hearer in a certain way. We may all hear a parable, but we do not all hear it the same way. The parable of the sower has many meanings, not only one.

First, let us take a different twist and look at the failure on the part of the sower. He threw some seeds on the wayside. He threw some on stony places. Some were tossed among the thorns and others on good ground.

Now we must stay with these seeds for a moment. It is, I submit, not a seed's fault if it does not grow properly on stony ground. It takes more than sun to grow. It takes good soil and moisture and time. See what I mean? The seed on the stony ground could not help itself. The fault must be placed here, if we are to place fault, either upon the nature of seeds in general or upon the sower for being so careless. The sower threw good seeds, we suppose, but did not throw them in the right places.

Let us pursue this line of thought. One year when I was in graduate school at Indiana University I was able to rent a garden plot. The deal was that the farmer, who owned the land, would plow it for us. He did. But he left clods so big that nothing would have grown there. I was able to break up some of the clods with a hoe and much muscle.

Now let us suppose I had been in a hurry and had simply scattered some seeds. What would have happened? Even if they had sprouted they would have been burnt up by the sun because they would not have been able to root in clods. True it takes good soil to grow seeds, but here we are still speaking of the sower's responsibility.

Like I had to break up the soil and prepare it, in a similar manner we Christian sowers have a responsibility to prepare the ground before throwing seeds around. I think that it is time we stopped blaming others if we are not doing our part. If you and I are going to be in the gospel business we must love those to whom we minister. And, if we are going to spread the seeds of the Christian "Good News" then it need be good news and not guilt trips. And we need patience and love in our message to others. I need to add the water a little at a time. You and I can trust God for the growth after we have done all the necessary preparation. Without preparation of the soil there will be no harvest.

Secondly, we turn our attention to the seed. We all know that any old kind of seed is not okay. You and I can not get corn from sunflower seeds, can we? The seeds need to be the right kind for the particular climate and soil conditions.

We have all seen signs in years past that say Jesus is the answer. That sounds good, but it is simplistic. Let us suppose someone is seeking the solution to three plus three. The answer here is not Jesus, it is six. We need to sow the Word of God in a responsible, mature manner. We must not be immature or silly as we do so.

If the Christian Gospel is the seed intended to be sown in this sophisticated world, then it has to be mature. We can expect results if we plant all the seed, not one-half of it. This seed needs to include a recognition of committed sins and repentance. The seed also includes God's grace and love. We have both the top and the bottom of the seed. I can not plant only half a seed and expect it to grow. Or if I am silly enough to expect it I will only be disappointed. I have to sow the entire seed.

Just as the sower has the responsibility to look after where and how he sows the seed, he also has a responsibility to use good, pure, and complete seeds. Some of us need to "study to show ourselves approved." In others words we need to do our homework before we go out into the fields.

Thirdly, there are different kinds of soil. And here the metaphor breaks down somewhat. I am old fashioned enough to think that the soil itself does also have a responsibility. This responsibility is to be as deep and as fertile as it can be. Some of us clods need to moisten up.

Now may we suppose for a moment that the congregation is like different types of soil? Jesus says there are four types:

1. the wayside type
2. the stony places type
3. the thorny type
4. the good ground type.

1. Jesus said that the first are those who do not understand the Word of the Kingdom (this means both himself and what he preaches). The evil one comes and snatches away even the little bit of seed that is sown in the heart. Of course, if

we are going to understand we must make an effort. We will need to read God's Holy Word and pray over it. And we will need to be open to God's surprises and new insights that he has in store for us as we grow and stretch beyond our present level of understanding. This sounds exciting doesn't it?

2. Jesus said that the second group are those who hear the Word and receive it with joy, but because this group has no root the Word only endures awhile. When tribulation comes the members of this group immediately stumble.

One man has said that the secret of success can be stated in nine words: "Stick to it, stick to it, stick to it." There are too many things started and not enough completed. A foreign language is learned one word at a time. An athlete must learn to move entire muscle groups a little at a time. A baseball batter swings time after time, for thousands of times (and strikes out many times) before he is ready for big league batting.

In the lexicon of youth there is no such word as "fail." Remember the story of the boy who wanted to march in the circus parade? When the show came to town, the bandmaster needed a trombonist, so the boy signed up. He had not marched a block before the fearful noises from his horn caused two older ladies to faint and a horse to run away. The bandmaster demanded, "Why didn't you tell me you couldn't play the trombone?" And the boy sweetly said, "How did I know? — I never tried before!"

3. The thorny type Jesus informed us is the one who hears the word, and the cares of this world and the deceitfulness of riches choke the Word, and this one becomes unfaithful.

Some people get off the track. When God's seed is sown it can start to take root but be choked out by all the things that we are concerned with from day to day. Self-pity can choke us away from God's optimism, mercy, and love for us. Our jobs, families and other interests can do this as well.

4. The fourth type is the type we all think we are — the good ground type. Jesus said that this good ground is the one who hears the Word and understands it.

In other words, the test of the good ground is that it produces. Sounds simple. A musician does not simply talk about playing music — she plays it. A runner runs. A Christian of the good ground type is expected to bear fruit, to tell others about Jesus Christ — and to help bring in the harvest for the Kingdom. Can you imagine how large our church buildings would have to be if we all did this? We wouldn't be able to build churches big enough. What a problem that would be!

Someone has said that the rest of the world is not interested in the storms we have encountered, but whether we brought in the ship. You and I need to stop making excuses and start scattering some seed around!

Let me share something that I recently read. It was originally published in the *Johnson County News* of Greenwood, Indiana: In 1923, a group of the world's most successful financiers met at the Edgewater Beach Hotel in Chicago. At this meeting were the following:

1. The president of the country's largest steel company.
2. The president of the country's largest utility company.
3. The greatest wheat speculator in the U.S.
4. The president of the New York Stock Exchange.
5. A member of the United States President's Cabinet.
6. The one known as the greatest "bear" on Wall Street.
7. The president of the Bank of International Settlements.
8. The head of one of the world's greatest monopolies.

It has been estimated that all these men together had more money than was in the United States Treasury at that time. For years newspapers and magazines had been printing their success stories and urging the youth of our country to follow in their examples. Here is what happened later to these men.

The president of the steel company, Charles Schwab, lived on borrowed money for the last five years of his life and died broke. The wheat speculator, Arthur Cutten, died abroad, insolvent. The president of the New York Stock Exchange, Richard Whitney, spent time at Sing Sing prison. The member of the President's Cabinet, Albert Fall, went to prison, then was pardoned so that he could die peacefully at home. The greatest "bear" of Wall Street, Jesse Livermore, committed suicide. The president of the Bank of International Settlements, Leon Fraser, committed suicide. The head of the world's greatest monopoly, Ivar Dreuger, committed suicide. All of these men had learned how to live well, as far as money goes, but none had learned to live a life with meaning.

It is important that we be good sowers so that more do not wind up like those mentioned. The Word of God is eternal. To obey this Word gives our lives meaning and hope. It is the pure seed, Jesus Christ, that should be and can be planted deep in the soil of our hearts. Let him who has ears hear: "He who sows the good seed is the Son of Man." (Matthew 13:37)

Matthew 13:24-30, 36-43 (C) Proper 11
Matthew 13:24-30, (36-43) (L) Pentecost 9
Matthew 13:24-43 (RC) Ordinary Time 16

Counterfeit Christians and the Rest of Us

Years ago at Park Rapids, Minnesota a tramp walked into a restaurant and asked the proprietor for a free meal. The hobo looked so hungry and bedraggled that the sympathetic restaurant man said, "O.K., what'll yuh have?" The tramp sat down at a table and had a good meal, a first class handout. As he was leaving, the hobo walked up to the proprietor and bummed a cigarette. He fished in a pocket for a match and along with the match he carelessly pulled out a twenty-dollar bill.

"Say, what's that," shouted the proprietor. "You come in here bumming a meal and you've got twenty bucks." And he grabbed the banknote.

"But this was supposed to be a free meal," the hobo protested.

"Not on your life," said the restaurant owner. "I'll just take the thirty-five cents out of this twenty."

"Just remember, buddy," said the tramp. "I don't want you to do this; I'm not asking you to do it."

"Is zat so," responded the restaurant man, and he handed the hobo nineteen dollars and sixty-five cents in change. The unhappy ending of the story for the proprietor was that when he took the money to the bank he found out that the twenty-dollar bill was counterfeit. He was then out not only one meal, but in his zeal to get what he thought he had coming he was out nearly twenty dollars as well.

The title of this sermon is "Counterfeit Christians and the Rest of Us." If you and I are busy seeing everyone else as fakes and we spend much of our time exposing their phoniness, then we do not have time to look at our own failures do we? Someone has said that if you have a fly in your eye, you cannot see that you have a fly in your eye. Jesus said that we do not see our own beams. This is why Jesus invited us to leave judgment up to God.

Jesus once told a parable. "The kingdom of heaven is like a man who sowed good seed in his field; but while the man slept, his enemy came and sowed tares among the wheat and went his way."

I'll bet that each one of us looks at a neighbor like a tare and see ourselves as wheat! In the newspaper this morning I read about the Sikh-Hindu rioting and killing in India, the looting of homes and killing in Pakistan and Iran, the problems in Sri Lanka between Tamils of the north and Buddhists of the south, and other such problems. This was all in one newspaper.

We have all read of Roman Catholic-Protestant conflicts (a religious war between different Christian groups) in Ireland, Iran-Iraq conflicts (a religious war between different Islamic groups), and the political unrest in South Korea (same nationality, different philosophies). Everyone seems to think that everyone else is the problem.

Many of us are so busy pulling out the tares in the field that we are destroying the world in the process. One commentator has said: "If we could cut down evil as the mower cuts the grass, if its forms all grew together, the field of the world could soon be cleared. But the intermixture of good and evil forbids rashness and haste."

Why do we not see the evil in our own lives? Why do we not all realize that not only are we far from being perfect, sometimes we are simply bad! It is like we have different personalities and each one fights to claim that it is lord of our souls. We are not good and others bad. We are all mixed wheat and tares. And until we see that and stop our judgment of others, until we stop fighting an enemy out there and not seeing the one within, there will not only fail to be peace in the world — there will be no peace in our own minds and hearts.

Personality theories in psychology may vary, but one thing they teach us is that there is an enemy, a counterfeit person, inside each one of us. And what is more, this counterfeit person tries to parade as the real us. How do we find out the real, God loved, soul inside each one of us? It is certainly not done by fighting what we assume to be enemies outside of us while denying the strife within.

In one congregation I served there was a man that had a disagreement with me. Yes, I said it right. I did not disagree with him. He disagreed with me as he had every minister before me, and perhaps every person he had ever known. Rather than give up membership in the church, he would come every Sunday then get up and leave as I began to preach. I tried reconciliation to no avail. Finally, I simply prayed about it and realized that he had the right to leave if he wanted. I did not see him as an enemy, nor do I judge him. But he certainly lived in more pain that he needed to live in. Maybe all disagreements are like that. And maybe we do not recognize our counterfeit selves.

Some of us are so counterfeit that the ink is still smudgy. This describes me at times. But then I am not all bad. Neither are you. Neither is your neighbor or mine! What we are instead are those poor, confused, self-righteous people, those stiff-necked people that Jesus came to minister to and to save. The good news is that even with our sin, even with our counterfeitedness (if that be a word), even with all the bad that is in us, still we were worth dying for in the loving eyes of Jesus Christ. That is tremendous when you stop to think about it.

Jesus Christ came to save us not only from destruction, but from each other and from our divided selves. He came to pull us away from condemnation and judgment of others. Christ wanted and still wants for us to let the good part inside of us to grow and to allow the bad part to slowly die. We can not simply tear out the bad in our minds and psyches and become saints over night. If we do we will do more damage than good. Instead, we have to slowly come to recognize that we do not have to identify with, and therefore give power to, those aspects of our own selves that can be called "tares."

Jesus taught us in today's parable that he and the angels will do the judging. Hear once more these words from Matthew 16:27: "For the Son of Man will come in the glory of His Father with His angels, and then He will reward each according to his works." This means that I do not have to worry about counterfeit others. If they are as truly bad as I have thought they were, then Christ will judge them. I can let go of judgment and with that let go of all the pain that those feelings cause me. I can stop being angry with others when I do not get my way or when they refuse to see things my way.

Here we must stop. Here we must point out that Jesus did take evil seriously. He taught very clearly that the world is a battle field where the forces of good and the forces of evil are engaged in complete, total conflict. But the enemy is not some imaginary person out there. It is our own divided selves. How dare we pass judgment on others when we fall short in so many ways ourselves?

But, finally, counterfeits teach us something else. If there is an imitation, then there must be a genuine counterpart. There are fake diamonds because there are real diamonds of great value. There is "fools gold" because there is real gold that is worthy of digging for in the earth. There are French names for American perfumes because the French have perfected perfume making.

Surely in the alchemical process of our dross being burned away we will discover that part of us that is not counterfeit. I can not be all imitation, nor can you. And it is that good part that Jesus wants to claim. And the good news is that we only have to leave the tares alone, not deny that they exist, but let them be and then God will uproot them and burn them up. In time, in God's own good time, we shall all be wheat and divided against ourselves and God no longer.

About the Author

Gary Houston has been a member of the North Indiana Conference of the United Methodist Church since 1980. Prior to that he taught Philosophy and World Religions at Ball State University. He has taught at Christian Theological Seminary, Indiana University at Kokomo, and at The School of Theology, the University of the South. He has published seven books that fall into the following divisions: two in Tibetan Studies, two on Christian-Buddhist Dialogue (editor), and three for CSS Publishing (sermons). He has written and published over a dozen articles and fifty book reviews on various subjects. He is a frequent contributor to *Emphasis* and has published sermons with Seabury Press and JLJ Publishing. His hobbies include computing, languages, and music. His wife Joyce puts up with it all.

www.ingramcontent.com/pod-product-compliance
Lightning Source LLC
Chambersburg PA
CBHW060852050426
42453CB00008B/959